Vietnam Travel Guide

Your Guidebook Trough Cities, Nature, Museums and Historical Monuments

Written by David Gordon

ISBN-13: 978-1541216303
ISBN-10: 154121630X

Table of Contents

History	1
Weather and Seasons	4
Northern Vietnam	5
Central Vietnam	6
Southern Vietnam	7
Cities to Visit	9
Hanoi	9
Hue	11
Hoi An	14
Da Lat	15
Ho Chi Minh City	17
Nature to See	19
Sapa	19
Ha Long Bay	21
Ninh Binh	23
Ho Chi Minh Road	25
Phong Nha Caves	26
Mui Ne beach	27
Mekong Delta	29
Museums to See	31
Hanoi – Hoa Lo Prison	31
Hoi An - My Son Ruins	32
Ho Chi Minh City - War Remnants Museum	33
Ho Chi Minh City - Cu Chi Tunnels	35
Local Specialties	37
Coffee	37
Pho noodles and beef	39
Final Words	42

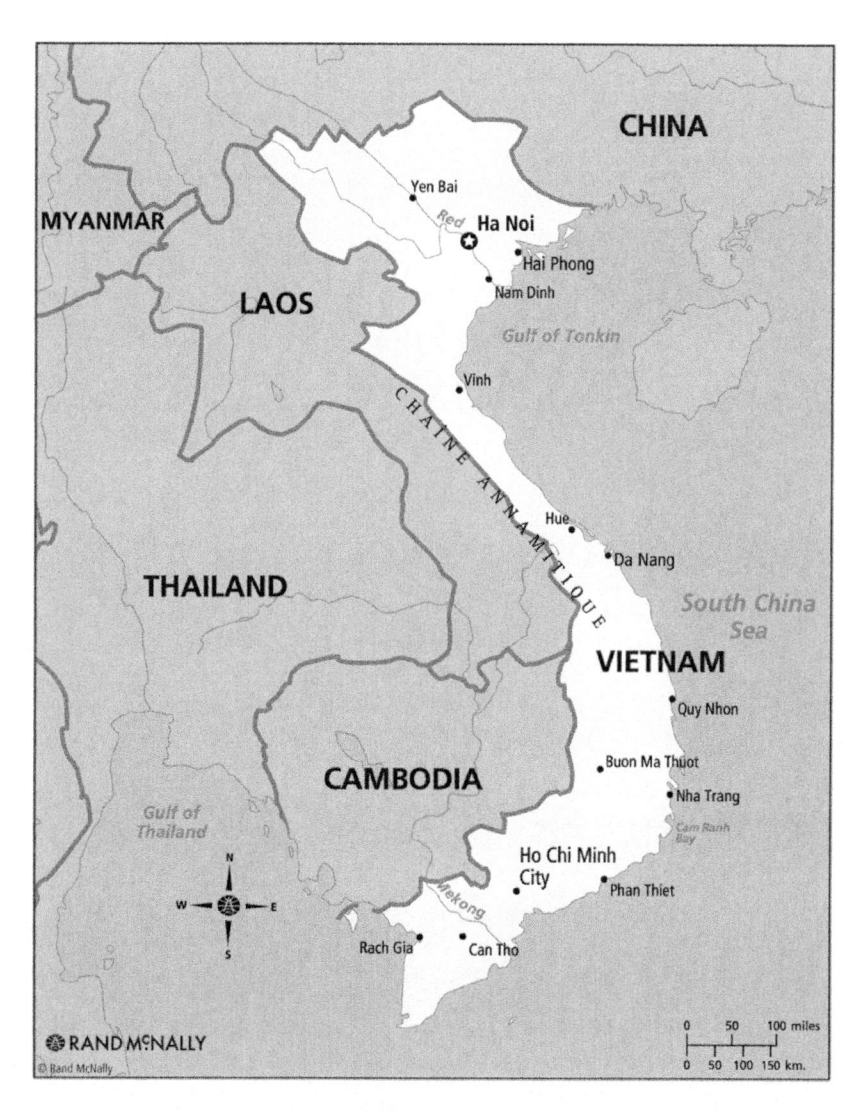

Map of Vietnam

History

Vietnam has a long and rich history characterized by Civil Wars, rebellion and colonization. According to archeological research, the earliest human habitation was recorded in the North 500,000 years ago where they used primitive tools to farm around the Red River Valley.

At around 2nd Century BC, an organized clan emerged called the Van Lang. Known for their famous culture of using sophisticated bronze tools and drums, the Van Lang kingdom was determined to build dykes and canals to irrigate their crops, especially rice.

However, after thousands of years of imperial dynasty, Vietnam was ravaged and divided by repeated attacks from the Chinese, the Songs, Mongols, Mings, French, Americans, Yuans, Dutch and the Chams. Although the Vietnamese rebelled and won most of these attacks, they remained to be subjects to Chinese rule until the French colonization.
From the 1st to the 6th centuries, Southern Vietnam was under the influence of Indians whom together formed the Cambodian Kingdom of Funan. The Funanese constructed a wall around the Cambodian Kingdom (modern day Tokeo) and constructed canal systems to act of highways to the great seas and also for irrigation of rice. According to archeologists, the port of Funan was a trade centre which attracted merchants from the west and the east.

During the 2nd Century AD, a Hindu kingdom known as the Champa emerged in the modern day Danang. Like Funan, the Champa borrowed most of the Indian culture, architect and adopted the Sanskrit language. As centuries went by, the Hindu kingdom continued to stretch towards the south to include bigger cities such as modern day Phan Rang and Nha Trang.

Northern Vietnam was conquered by China in the 2nd century. This saw a large number of Chinese settlers, scholars and officials move to the North to impose the Chinese state system to the Vietnamese. Since the local rulers were not satisfied with the Chinese rule, there where resistant groups such as the famous Trung Sisters (Hai Ba Trung). Calling themselves the Queens of Independent Vietnam, the Trung Sisters led a revolt army which fought for freedom forcing the Chinese governor and other officials to flee. However, in AD 43, the Trung Sisters were counterattacked forcing them to kill themselves instead of suffering the ignominy of surrender.

After a long Chinese dynasty in the South, a leader Ngo Quyen led a rebellion and conquered the Chinese army on a battle in the Bach Dang River. From the 11th to the 13th century, Vietnam was independent with power being filled by emperors of the Ly Dynasty. Throughout the independence error, Vietnam faced a lot of external attacks from the Chinese, the Cham and the Khmer.

During the 17th and the 18th century, the Ly Dynasty ended and Vietnam was taken over by two rival families; the Trinh in the North and Nguyen in the South.

In 1765, the Nguyen Brothers led a rebellion in the city of Tay Son near Qui Nhon and took control of central Vietnam. In 1783, the brothers went ahead to reap the Nguyen Lords off the leadership over South Vietnam killing all the lords and their families. Nguyen Lu was crowned emperor over South Vietnam while Nguyen Nhac was crowned king over Central Vietnam. Taking advantage of the strength and dynasty of the Nguyen family, the third Nguyen brother conquered the Northern Empire overthrowing the Trinh lords and crowning himself emperor Quant Trung.

Starting from the 19th to late 20th century, Vietnam became subjects to European power such as France and the U.S.A. Vietnam engaged in guerilla wars from this time throughout 1940s till 1973 when a cease-fire agreement was reached. Throughout the Vietnam war, an estimated 3 million Vietnamese and over 55,000 American soldiers were killed in battle.

Today, Vietnam is among the fastest growing economies in the world recording an annual growth of 8%. In 1994, U.S. forged diplomatic relations with Vietnam with President Bill Clinton being the first American President to visit Northern Vietnam. With a fast-growing economic growth and various tourist attractions, Vietnam has a bright future of success both politically and economically. In 2016 President Barrack Obama visited Vietnam.

Obama eating in typical restaurant in Hanoi

Weather and Seasons

When planning to visit Vietnam, weather and seasons are some of the basic factors to consider. Following the country's 2000+ miles of coastline from the North in Hanoi to the South in Ho Chi Minh City, the country experiences mixed weather and seasons. For instance, the North and the South experiences Tropical monsoon climate and sunshine along the beaches while the Mountainous far North of Sapa experiences snow and cold weather.

Knowing the best times to visit Vietnam is very essential. The Southern parts of Vietnam which consists of Ho Chi Minh City and Phu Quoc are characterized with dry monsoon climate from May to September. The cold monsoon winds gathers moisture from the Gulf of Tonkin and takes it to the Central highlands and the mountainous far North of Hanoi, Halong Bay, Mai Chau, Sapa, Ha Giang and Bac Ha. The cold weather is mostly experienced in December and January while the Central Highlands remains cool throughout the year.

Northern Vietnam

Climate in Northern Vietnam as well as in the Mountainous far North is warm and sunny from October to April, wet from May to September. In Northern Vietnam in parts like Hanoi, Halong Bay, Mai Chau, Cuc Phuong and Ninh Binh dry winter is experienced from November to April with temperatures ranging from 60 to 75°F (17-22°C). Summer lasts from May to October while heavy downpour is experienced from July to September.

The Mountainous far North in parts like Sapa, Bac Ha and Ha Giang experiences dry seasons from October to late March with the rainy seasons lasting from April to September. The winter season ranges from December to January with daytime temperatures ranging from 60 to 65°F (15-28°C) while at night temperatures range from 50 to 60°F 10-18°C.

When visiting the northern Mountainous parts of Vietnam for trekking and cycling, come during summer and winter seasons (November to April) as climate is dry and quite cold(er). Avoid travelling during cold seasons as some parts such as Ha Giang may be characterized with bad weather or floods.

Central Vietnam

The central regions of Vietnam experiences both dry and wet weather throughout the year. Hot weather starts from April to late September with temperatures reaching as high as 85°F (30°C). From January to July, these parts experience minimal rain while in September to December, heavy rainfall and colder weather take over.

When paying a visit in Hue, it's wise to go during summer (January to August) so you can take advantage of the mountains. Hoi An is quite similar to Hue but its proximity to the Southern system makes it experience longer dry seasons than Danang and Hue.

As you stretch far south of central Vietnam, you'll find Nha Trang which is a dry region with typical high temperatures from January to September. The rainy season is only experienced from September to early December. Although the central region is characterized with shorter rainy seasons and long dry seasons, these regions are mostly hit by typhoons and hurricane-winds which last from August to November.

Southern Vietnam

With lack of mountains in the south, the climate in this part is split into two seasons namely wet and dry.

The dry season starts on December and goes through April to late May. The rainy season then starts from mid-May and goes all the way through to November.

During the dry season, temperatures go as high as 100°F (40°C) from November to April. At this time, the best places to visit is Phu Quoc, Dalat and Ho Chi Minh City.

The wet season starts from May to November but heavy downpour is experienced from June to August. During these months, floods are experienced in the lower parts of the Mekong Delta with heavy rains being seen in the afternoon. Daytime temperatures range at 70°F (20°C) while temperatures are quite cold at night 50°F (9°C). The monsoon winds in the South causes flooding in Saigon and makes transport more complicated in southern Island of Phu Quoc.
Below follows a graph which displays the weather from north to south. There really is no perfect time to visit Vietnam because it's 2000 miles from north to south which leads to significant differences in climate.

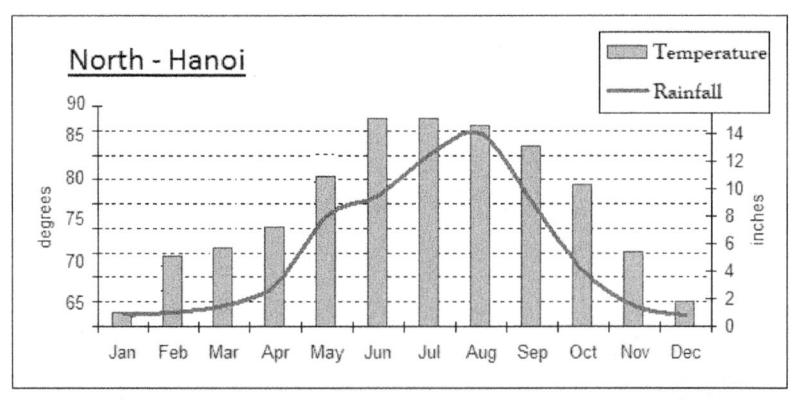

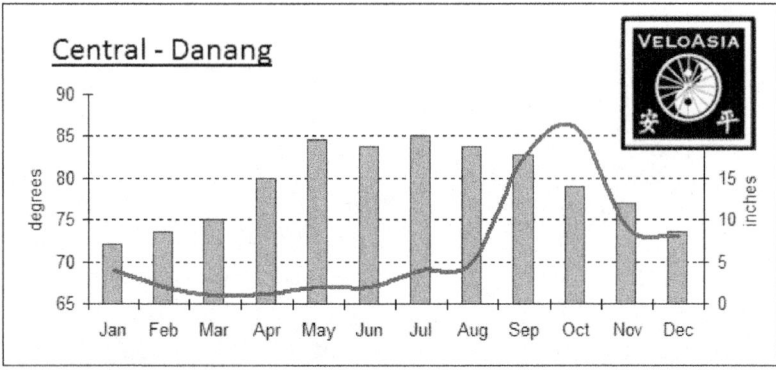

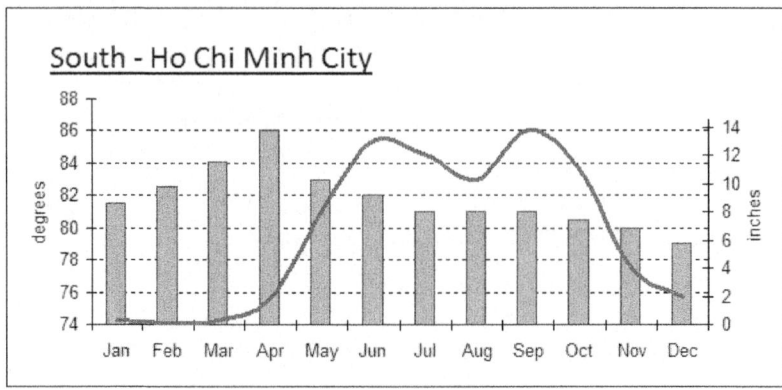

Weather in Vietnam

Cities to Visit

There are beautiful cities to explore in Vietnam. In the less developed cities you will find authentic building styles. The building style will vary from Vietnamese to French. In this overview of cities, we will follow cities from North to South.

Hanoi

Hanoi is the second largest and also the capital city of Vietnam. The city has been in existence since the 2nd century and has currently achieved an estimated population of 7.7 million people. A city with a long political history, Hanoi served as the capital during the French rule from 1902 to 1954. Served as a political centre from 1010 to 1802 and served as an imperial capital during the Nguyen Dynasty from 1802 to 1945 before being declared the Vietnam's capital in 1976.

Hanoi is located in the Northern region of Vietnam near the Red River Delta. The city is 55 miles (90 km) away from the coastal area with a mountainous terrain surrounding it from east to west. The city experiences four distinct climates which include; summer (from May-August) characterized with hot sun and moderate rainfall, heavy rainfall with decrease in temperature (from September—October) and winter season from November to January.

Hanoi experiences an average rainfall of 1,680 milliliters per year. It has an average temperature of 75°F (23.6°C) and an average humidity of 79%.

As the capital city of Vietnam for almost 1,000 years, Hanoi has been a converging centre for many European (French), Indian and local cultures. Starting with the native Vietnamese dynasties, the Indian Funanese and the French, the city has been left with imprints, interesting cultures and historical monuments which teach us more about the historic events and form of life.

Nicknamed *"City of Lakes"*, Hanoi lies between many lakes which are the reason for its cool weather and scenic beauty. Among these great lakes that are in the city include; the West Lake, Hoan Kiem Lake (also known as Sword Lake) and the Bay Mau Lake. Along the lakes, there are many temples, bars and bicycling areas where tourist and the local people can spend time together watching the majestic Westlake sunset.

Sunset at Westlake

Hanoi is home to a number of famous museums and historical monuments. Among these museums include; Vietnam Museum of Revolution, Hoa Lo Prison, Ho Chi Minh Museum, Vietnam Military History Museum and Vietnam Nation Museum of Fine Art. The city has a picturesque outlook with the metropolis being named the Paris of the East. In 2015, Hanoi was ranked the 4th leading tourist destination by TripAdvisor.

Streets of Hanoi

Hue

An old city in Central Vietnam whose origin dates back to the 1800s, Hue was named as the country's capital during the Nguyen Dynasty. The city lies about 700 km south of Hanoi, 1,100 km north of Ho Chi Minh City and just a few miles from the coast. Hue was the capital of Vietnam from 1802-1945.
The history of Hue exists of war and rebellion. The reason why the city was so prone to sabotage and frequent attacks was due to its geographical location where it bordered the north and south territories.
When you visit Hue, you'll notice that most parts of the city are occupied with damaged buildings, complex structures, tombs and pagodas which signify the existence of exotic cultures and feudal empires.

Emperor Tombs - most of the Nguyen emperors' tombs were scattered along the Perfume River. Among the emperors buried along this central region include; Minh Mang, Tu Duc and Dong Khanh.

Hue Citadel - located in the northern sides of Perfume River, the citadels comprise of shrines, palaces and the forbidden Purple City where tourists and residents can visit and relax. It only takes half a day to tour the entire complex.

Hue Citadel

Pagodas - common in most songs and poems, the Thien Mu Pagoda is an essential part of Hue city which tourists can't miss to visit. Commonly known for its octagonal 12-meter high tower, the pagoda combines ancient architectural art and picturesque nature which attracts tourists from all over the globe. Other pagodas around this city where visitors can tour include; Tu Dam, Huyen Khong and Tu Hieu.

Due to the Bach Ma Mountain that lies 37 miles (60 km) south of the city, Hue city experiences four seasons with a tropical monsoon climate. The dry season starts from March to August with temperatures ranging from 95 to 105°F (35-40°C). The rainy season is experienced from August to January while heavy downpour which causes floods is experienced in October. During the rainy season, temperatures rise as high as 68 and as low as 50°F (20 to 9°C).

Other activities which tourists can enjoy in Hue City during summer include relaxing on the beautiful beaches of Thuan An and Lang Co while viewing the blue ocean and playing with the white silky sand.

Thuan An Beach

Hoi An

Hoi An is an old city with a very long history. It's located in Central Vietnam along the coast of the Vietnam Central Sea. With approximately 120,000 inhabitants, Hoi An is a town inhabited with mixed ancient architect dating back to the 15th - 19th century. According to many, the city was a centre of trade and influences of Western, Asian and local relations and existence have been reflected with the buildings and streets plan around the city.
During the 1st century, Hoi An was known as the Champa City. The people of Champa controlled the harbor and were in charge of the spice trade which made them so wealthy. Throughout the 16th and the 17th centuries, the Chinese, the Dutch, the Indians and the Japanese became frequent trade associates with some settling permanently in the area.

In 1999, Hoi An was recognized by UNESCO as a World Heritage Site due to its well preserved history and reputation. The city homes numerous ancient temples, pagodas, buildings and art with a blend of both foreign and local influence. The history of the city such as the prosperous merchant past and progress, are well depicted and documented both in writing and in priceless relics.

Hoi An has four major museums which highlight the city's history. Among them include the **Museum of History and Culture** which was once a pagoda build in the 17th century by local Minh Huong villagers to warship Quan An. This museum contains the history of the early settlers of Hoi An city from the Champa, Dai Viet, Sa Huynh, the locals and the French colonialists.

The other three museums comprise of Hoi An **Folklore Museum**, the Museum of **Trade Ceramics** and Museum of **Sa Huynh Culture**. All these three museums are displayed with ancient artifacts and antiques which signify trade relations between the local inhabitants and the Chinese, the Persians, Indians and Thailand.

The best time to visit Hoi An is during the summer season from end May to end August when the sea is calm.

Da Lat

Da Lat is a city located in the South Central Highlands of Vietnam. With an estimated population of 210 thousand people, the city of Da Lat is 4,900 ft above sea level on the Langbian Plateau.

Due to its cool temperatures all year round, the French colonialists found Da Lat to be an ideal and strategic point to build a city. In 1907, urban planning began with the construction of the first hotel while by 1920s, the French endowed the city with villas, parks, schools, golf courses, health complexes and boulevards.

Currently, Da Lat is a popular tourist attraction in Vietnam characterized with ancient buildings and art bearing French and Normandy architect. The city is characterized with pine wood, twisting roads and picturesque scenery which are highly attractive especially at night. Its cool weather makes the city a strategic place for research in the fields of biotechnology. Agriculture is another economic activity on the rise in this area. Due to the cool temperatures, Vietnamese Government has set up cabbage, cauliflower and fruits (strawberry, mulberry and sweet potato) industries which add up in the country's economy.

Among the best places you're expected to tour when you get to Vietnam include;

The Three Palaces - built during the colonial era by emperor Bao Dai. The three palaces which are named Palace I, II and III have become a major tourist attraction in the city.

The Crazy House - which was built by the daughter of a French Governor is another tourist attraction in the area.

Other areas where visitors can tour include; the Huan Huong Lake, the Da Lat Market, the Lang Bien Mountain, Lake of Sorrow, Thung Lung Tinh Yeu (the Valley of Love), Da Lat Train Station, a ride on top of Lang Biang Mountain as well as Prenn Falls, Pongour Falls and Elephant Falls.
There are lots of **waterfalls** around the area which makes this place the best place in Vietnam to do Kayaking & Canoeing.

DaLat Crazy House

Ho Chi Minh City

Ho Chi Minh City is the largest city in Vietnam also referred to as Saigon. With an estimated area of 30,000 sq km, the city has 5 rural districts and 19 urban cities.
Ho Chi Minh City has been in existence as long as history can remember. It has gone by different names which reflect the settlement of different ethnic groups throughout history. Originally a swampland inhabited by the Khmer People, Ho Chi Minh City was given as a dowry to the Vietnamese government after the marriage between the Khmer Prince and Vietnamese Princess.
From the 1600s, the city became a subject to the Nguyen Dynasty rule before the Franco-Spanish forces attack in 1859.

Ho Chi Minh City is located 1100 miles (1760 km) south of Hanoi at an elevation of 62 ft above sea level. It has a tropical wet and dry climate with an average humidity of 78-82%. The year is divided into two seasons which include the rainy season from May to October and the dry season from December to April.

There are many French colonial historic buildings in Ho Chi Minh City. Most of these historic structures are located in District 1 and just a short distance from each other. Among these structures include; the **Reunification Palace**, the **Municipal Theater** (also known as the Opera House), the **State Bank Office** and the **Notre-Dame Cathedral**.

Ho Chi Minh City Skyline with the Notre-Dame

The city also boasts some of the best historic hotels such as Hotel Majestic, the Rex and Caravelle hotels. Among the notable museums in Ho Chi Minh City include; Museum of Vietnamese History, Ho Chi Minh City Museum, the **War Remnants Museum**, the Revolutionary Museum, the Museum of Fine Art and the **Cu Chi Tunnels**.

Aside from the museums, the city has numerous places of entertainment which has boosted the number of visitors touring the area to approximately 4 million annually. The Ben Thanh theatre, Hoa Binh theatre and Lan Anh Music Stage are among the famous drama and cinema theatres in the region.

Nature to See

Vietnam is a country with a lot of beautiful nature. People don't come for the museums and cities alone. The good thing is that this nature is widely open to tourists who want to explore the beauty of Vietnam. Again The activities are listed from north to south.

Sapa

Sapa is a city located in the remote mountainous regions along the Chinese Vietnam border at a place known as *"the Tonkinese Alps"*. With a height of 1500m (4921ft) above sea level this area gets quite cold especially at night. There are many famous natural sceneries and rich cultural diversity around Sapa. The surrounding region is mostly inhabited by many hill tribes such as the Black Hmong people and the Giay people.

Beautiful hills of Sapa

Let's look at some of the things to do in Sapa.

Cat Cat Village - this is the first destination you're expected to land when beginning your trip to Sapa. Located only 3km from Sapa, the Cat Cat Village has picturesque scenery of beautiful roses and rice plantation. Around the visibility, you'll be expected to view the Golden River, the Love Waterfall and the Silver Waterfall.

Four kilometers down the valley, you'll come across Sin Chai Village, the home to Black Hmong people as well as the Ta Van Village of the Giay people. During tour seasons, visitors are given a chance to learn the different cultures and costumes of the two native tribes.

Ta Phin Village - at just 17km in the west of Sapa lays Ta Phin village. Inhabited by local Red Dao's people, this village is quite indigenous and is possessed by the original Vietnamese culture which has not been diluted by modern influence.

As you get closer to the villages, you'll discover women and children weaving colorful bags, scarfs, backpacks and skirts using large balls of thread. Apart from selling their woven stuff to tourists and other local visitors, the Red Dao's people sell their supply for export to other countries.

Hoang Yen Chao Castle - Hoang Yen Chao Castle is a unique architectural structure built during the 20th century. With a combination of the Eastern and Western architecture, this structure was built as a residence and fortress for Huong Yen Chao and his son Huong A Tuong. This unique castle and defending tower for that matter was built with high fences, deep trenches and blockhouses to ensure that enemies had no chance to get through its threshold.

Ham Rong Mountain - this is one of the must-see attraction sites for tourists visiting Sapa. Also known as Dragon Jaw, Ham Rong Mountain has a combination of man-made and natural landscapes which makes it a spectacular site for most tourists.

Ha Long Bay

Located in the province of Quang Ninh, Ha Long Bay is scenery full of unimaginable beauty and picturesque landscapes. The bay stretches 120 km along the coastline and is approximately 1,553 sq km in size. There are lots of natural scenery along the bay which makes it one of the major tourist attractions in Vietnam. There are hundreds of limestone karsts and isles, enormous caves, floating villages, spectacular pillars along the coast line and natural islands which lay uninhabited.

Ha Long Bay

Other outstanding scenic beauties tourists are expected to enjoy in Ha Long Bay include:

Dau Be Island - located 500m east of Hang Trai Island and south of Ha Long Bay, Dau Be Island has a total area of 22,863m sq. The Island is silent and stands between natural cliffs which shield it against the cold waves running from the east into the gulf.
Dau Be Island is among the famous tourist attraction sites in Vietnam due to its magnificent picturesque scenery. There, you'll find the B Ham Lake which meanders through a large cave. There are hundreds of species of orchids, banyans and palm trees and is a home to the golden monkeys, birds and squirrels.

Bo Hon Island - Bo Hon Island is one of the most famous tourist attractions in Ha Long Bay. As one of the largest Islands, Bo Hon is famous for its chain of spectacular caves such as Tien Cave, Trinh Nu Cave, Luon Cave and Trong Cave.
Besides the magnificent caves system, this Island is home to thousands of species of plants such as Banyan Trees and animals such as monkeys, antelopes and deer.

Lan Ha Bay—located just a few miles from Ha Long Bay; Lan Ha Bay is another famous tourist attraction with about 400 small and large islands. Temperatures around the silk white beaches are convenient for swimming while trees and green vegetation gives the limestone cliffs an amazing view. Lan Ha Bay has 139 clean beaches, caves and is a home to hundreds of species of wild animals such as monkeys.

Ninh Binh

Located just 100 km south of Hanoi along the Red River Delta, Ninh Binh is emerging as one of the most exciting tourist destinations in Vietnam. Formerly known as the shortest route to Hanoi, this city now features some spectacular karst scenery which every tourist can't imagine missing out. There are two ways which tourists can use to get to Ninh Binh. You can either board a bus at just $4 from Giap Bus Station or a train from Hanoi. This section will review some of the many scenery, nature and things to do in Ninh Binh.

The Halong Bay - the Halong Bay is one of the most interesting places to tour once you visit Ninh Binh City. Taking a boat ride through an extensive network of waterways between erected limestone cliffs will take you through Trang An, Tam Coc, Bich Dong Temple and three caves Hang Ca 127m high, Hang Giua 70m high and Hang Cuoio 40m high.

Around the river, there are small floating stalls where you can buy food and drinks. The area around Ngo Dong River is suitable for tourists who enjoy cycling and walking. You can hire a bike, walk or use a boat to enjoy the magnificent landscape around the hills and ever-green fields.

"The Halong Bay" in Ninh Binh

The ancient capital Hoa Lu - just a few miles from Ninh Binh City, you'll get to Hoa Lu town. Known for its exclusive temples with cultural assets, this royal city is surrounded with Limestone Mountains which acted as defense against invaders. Among the temples standing in this world heritage site include the temple of Dinh Tien Hoang who liberated Vietnam from the southern Han during the 10th century.

Cuc Phuong National Park - Cuc Phuong is the oldest national park in Vietnam located 30 km west of Ninh Binh. As a natural rainforest, Cuc Phuong Natural Park is a home to over 150 species of primates and plants. There are different ways through which tourists can explore the park. You can either travel by bus, motorbike, by boat or hire a bike. Cuc Phuong National Park has plenty of caves and is home to many species of butterflies and birds.

Ho Chi Minh Road

Ho Chi Minh Road is a 2000km trail that runs from Saigon in the south to Hanoi in the north. Famous during the Vietnam War, this scenic route has fast become a major tourist attraction due to the numerous sites and landscapes which lay along the visibility. The road has fully been paved and features beautiful scenes such as clear blue rivers, tropical rainforests, spectacular landscapes and endless limestone mountains which stretches to the horizon. Taking a motorbike tour through this trail gives you a chance to experience the beauty of Vietnam from its core. Here is a small guide of what you'll experience during your tour along Ho Chi Minh Road.

Ho Chi Minh road

northern part—the northern part covers a distance of 450km running from Pho Chau—Tan Ky--Cam Thuy—Cuc Phuong—Hanoi. Along this area, there are lots of sceneries to enjoy such as the Coc Phuong National Park, the Turquoise Buoi River, cement factories, limestone hills and mysterious landscapes which are commonly used for shooting Hollywood movies.

Central part—the central part has a distance of 280km and runs from Kon Tum—Kham Duc—Prao. Around this section, you'll come across towering rubber trees, coffee bushes, forest regions and finally the Ngoc Linh Mountain (the highest mountain in Central and South Vietnam with a height of 2,598m).

Southern part—the southern part is split into two sections. The first section has a distance of 340km and runs from Saigon—Dong Xoai—Gia Nghia—Buon Ma Thuot. When starting your journey from Saigon, you'll pass over the clogged Binh Trieu Bridge through the Saigon industrial belt. You'll pass through the Binh Duong New City and head your way towards Dong Xoai.
From Dong Xoai, you'll get to Gia Nghia, an old city that's perched on top of a red soil hillside. Here, you'll find old monuments of government offices, empty boulevards and finally a large hydroelectric power project. The old town has plenty of fascinating activities from the locals with delicious dishes and decent hotels to spend the night.
From Gia Nghia to Boun Ma Thuot, you'll pass through farms and plantations which were formerly forested regions. This desolate region gives you the memories of the Vietnam War where American aircrafts heavily bombed the region to break connections between the north and south.

Phong Nha Caves

Phong Nha is fast becoming a tourist attraction following a number of natural scenery and beauty. Tourists who visit this region have a great chance to see the Phong Nha Caves (Paradise Cave) which have become a natural wonder of Vietnam.

Phong Nha Ke Bang National Park - opened to public in 2010, this national park consists of untouched beauty which spreads all along the rugged landscape. The park has numerous large caves such as the famous Paradise Cave, Hang En cave, Son Doong cave and Phong Nha cave.

Tu Lan cave - these caves are some of the most beautiful untouched regions of Vietnam. There you'll enjoy the scenery of real jungles, rivers, waterfalls and historic cultures of the minorities. There are a number of underground rivers and many species of birds and bats living inside the caves.

Hang Son Doong - discovered as the largest cave in the world in 2009, Hang Son Doong is located in a spectacular region characterized with beautiful jungles and ever green valleys. There are lots of adventures lying inside the cave but the most amazing fact is its magnificent size which can fit an entire city including skyscrapers. During the season (from February to August), tourists visiting this area are restricted to only 10. You need to reserve spots for this cave a few years in advance and tickets are not cheap.

Mui Ne beach

Mui Ne Beach is a precious gift of nature located 5-6 hours from Ho Chi Minh City (by bus) and less than an hour from Phan Thiet District. Mui Ne Beach features a series of beaches such as Ong Dia Beach, the Front Beach and the Back Beach. There are many sceneries and interesting sites along this area such as colored sand-dunes, tropical rainforests, waterfalls, coral reefs, exotic beaches, caves and bamboo forests among many others. With few people living around these areas, the government of Vietnam has played a key role of ensuring that the Mui Ne Beach is cherished and protected from pollution and unnecessary exploitation. Here are a few things you'll see and enjoy in this area.

The Beach at Mui Ne

Sand hills - one of the wonders of nature you'll see in Mui Ne beach are the sand dunes which gather together to form tall hills of colored sand. These hills are also known as flying sand dunes because they change the shape hourly, weekly or monthly depending with the speed of the wind. Viewing the sand dunes early in the morning at around 5:30am gives you a spectacular picture of the surrounding characterized with green vegetation and golden sand dunes.

The Cham Towers is another historically interesting scenery around Mui Ne beach. Built around the 8th century as temple complex, they offer a great spot to catch the sunset as you view the picturesque scenery of Phan Thiet City.

Due to the high temperatures around Mui Ne beach, there are lots of interesting activities around the beach such as swimming, scuba diving, sailing, sight-seeing and sun-bathing among others. There are numerous delicious sea-foods and local beach festivals which tourists can enjoy.

Mekong Delta

Vietnam has two major deltas which include the Red River Delta and the Mekong Delta. This region is formed by the great Mekong River which traverses a total of 4,500km from China through Burma, Laos, Thailand to Southern Vietnam. According to the Vietnamese, Mekong is also referred to as Cuu Long which means *"nine dragons"*. This name was given due to Mekong River's nine exit points as it flows to the sea.
Mekong's delta offers a variety of tourist attractions and activities which visitors can enjoy. Nature's lovers can tour through the small villages, along the rice fields or tour the floating market with abundance of fruits and vegetables.

Can Tho - Can Tho is one of the major tourist attractions in Mekong Delta. There are many floating markets and huge streets along this area where visitors can purchase locally made fabrics, ice-creams, fruits, snacks and different species of fish. The two major markets in this area are Cai Rang and Phung. While the former sells a variety of fruits and vegetables, the latter is famous for selling different species of poisonous snakes such as pythons, cobras and black mamba among others.

Mountain Sam - also referred to as the *"Holy"* mountain, Mountain Sam is another major tourist destination in Mekong Delta. There are many caves, shrines and temples across the region. This area attracts more devotees, tourists and vendors during the annual Ba Chu Xu religious festivals.

Con Phung Island - Con Phung is a familiar island in Mekong Delta with numerous tourist attractions cross the landscape. The island was also known as *"the Island of the Coconut Monk"* following a tale of monk Ong Dao Dua who stayed in the island for three years meditating while eating coconuts. Ong Dao Dua is remembered for his attempts to reunify Vietnam through peaceful means and a cross (which resembles a swastika) is found in his sanctuary which symbolizes his victory over the communist community.

Mekong delta

Museums to See

Hanoi – Hoa Lo Prison

Located in the lower parts of Hanoi city, Hoa Lo Prison is one of the most infamous museums surrounded with sorrow, disgust and horrifying scenery. Built in the early 20th century by French colonialists to detain and torture Vietnamese political prisoners, Hoa Lo Prison was later used as an interrogation centre as well as a prison by Vietnam government during the American War.

Previously designed to hold a maximum of 400 prisoners, the number drastically grew to 2,000 with majority of them being political prisoners. After independence, the Vietnam Government thought of preserving the prison as a reminder but plans changed during the Vietnam War and the prison was once again used to detain American POWs. According to American survivors such as POW Julius Jayroe, James Stockdale, Gen. Robinson Risner and 2008 Presidential nominee John McCain, Hoa Lo Prison was a real hell. Although the Vietnamese government states that American prisoners were well-treated, sources from former inmates reveal that there was murder, torture and medical neglect.

From 1990s, the government of Vietnam demolished part of the prison and sold the land to investors who built hotels and other business structures. A portion of the prison was preserved and named Hoa Lo Prison museum.

On the entrance to the museum, you'll find its original name Maison Centrale meaning the *"Central House"*. During the French rule, the Vietnamese prisoners nick-named it *"the Monster's Mouth"* while the Americans nicknamed it *"the Hanoi Hilton"*. Moving through the torture chambers, you'll find an array of horrifying shackles, whips, John McCain's flight suit and a guillotine used to make an end at the prisoner's life.

Hoi An - My Son Ruins

My Son is a UNESCO World Heritage Site located just 50km from the beautiful Port City. Established during the 4th to the 13th centuries AD, My Son was the home to the Champa people also known as the Champa Kingdom. The complex is located on the mountains of Quang Nam Province in Central Vietnam. My Son is placed in a geographical basin surrounded with numerous mountains which are the source to Thu Bon River.

A part of the My Son ruins

Ruled by the Champa kings from the 3rd century to 1832, My Son became a complex mixed with Indian Hinduism and local influence. The Champa people, who were predominantly Hindus, built numerous temples and statues of Vishnu, Shiva and Krishna to demonstrate their faith. The earliest temples were made of wood but as time elapsed, the Champa kings rebuilt the temples to include bricks and limestone.

Unfortunately, during the Vietnam war, My Son was heavily bombed by U.S. bombers following propaganda that the Viet Cong had moved to the complex to use it as a military base. Since the buildings were not strongly structured, most of them received substantial damage. Today, reconstruction of the temples is underway and the government is using the same exact materials and architect used by the Champa people.

There are lots of structures decorated with sculptures of sacred animals, mythical gods, priests, various kings who ruled Champa Kingdom as well as scenes of mythical battles. When you enter the park, you'll see a dusty walking path which leads you through the ruins. There, you'll view all the 8 groups of temples and 71 standing monuments which lie desolate and forgotten. A walkway through the jungle underbrush will lead you towards the small rest areas, toilets and souvenir shops where you can purchase some items.

Ho Chi Minh City - War Remnants Museum

When you visit Ho Chi Minh City, one of the destinations you can't afford to miss out is the War Remnants Museum. Operated by the Vietnamese government, the War Remnants Museum was officially opened on September 1975 as a home to display war crimes and other American fire-powers during the Vietnam War.

A Helicopter used by the United States in the war

The war equipment displayed in War Remnants Museum date back to 1858 when the French first attacked Vietnam. After being declared an independent country under President Ho Chi Minh, the United States sparked another war which is mostly referred to as the *"the U.S. War"* or the *"U.S. Aggressive War in Vietnam"* by the Vietnamese.

Although Vietnam may have won the war against the United States, the War Remnants Museum documents the cost of war through shore casing the machines and technology used by the Americans. Among the military equipment you'll see in this museum include; the F-111 bomber jet, tanks, war planes and Chinook helicopters. Along the walls of the museum, there are disturbing pictures of the My Lai massacre, the guillotine used to prosecute prisoners and the traumatizing consequences of the phosphorus bombs and Agent Orange. War Remnants Museum doesn't just tell the painful tales of the Vietnam War but it also illustrates the untold stories about the war through display of deadly military equipment and photographs taken by photographers during the war.

As a matter of fact, most western tourists who tour this area have failed to hold their tears when they see the disturbing photos, tiger cages and guillotine machine used during war. This museum is well worth the visit because it displays the war through the eyes of the Vietnamese people instead of the Americans.

Ho Chi Minh City - Cu Chi Tunnels

Cu Chi Tunnels is another tourist attraction in south Vietnam. Located about 40km northwest of Ho Chi Minh City (Saigon), these series of tunnels were dug beneath the Cu Chi district at approximately 250km.

Digging the tunnels first began in late 1940s in the jungle terrain of South Vietnam during the French colony. In early 1960s after the Americans escalated its military presence in South Vietnam in support of a non-communist regime, the Viet Cong and North Vietnamese troops joined forces and expanded the tunnels to all their districts from Cu Chi district through Saigon to the Cambodian border.

The Cu Chi tunnels provided shelter to most civilians who were victims of war. There were kitchens, hospitals to nurse injured soldiers, bomb shelters, music halls and living areas for the Cu Chi people. Since the U.S. troops heavily relied on aerial bombing, the Viet Cong and North Vietnamese troops would disappear below the ground and lay surprise attacks to the American soldiers. There were numerous booby traps laid by the VC troops such as planting trip wires which would detonate grenades and overturn boxes loaded with poisonous snakes and scorpions on the enemy heads.

One of the booby traps

Currently, visitors touring the Cu Chi Tunnels can see the booby traps used during war, the type of lifestyle the local Cu Chi people used to live as well as the remnant bomb craters which will remind you of the B-52 bombers dropped during the Operation Cedar Falls. There are numerous automatic rifles such as AK-47, M-16, M-60, M1 carbine and Russian SKS which you can pay to fire some bullets at the firing range. You can expect to pay around $15 to shoot 10 rounds with an AK-47.

Local Specialties

Although most people may suggest that Thai food is the most heralded of all the South Asian foods, Vietnam has the most astonishing varieties of flavored cuisines in the entire Asian region. What makes the local specialties so special is due to a mix of local, French, Indian and Thai influences. Most of the Vietnamese dishes are boiled, streamed or seasoned with herbs rather than being fried. Among the various foods and drinks which tourists can enjoy in Vietnam include; sea food, vegetarian food, beef, fruits, rice wine, lime soda, herbal tea and of course coffee.

Coffee

Vietnamese coffee is one of the best in the world. As the second largest coffee producing country in the world, Vietnam has managed to offer its visitors a chance to taste a variety of good tasting coffee both in the restaurants and street cafes. Most visitors touring Vietnam have praised the sweetened condensed milk mixed with robust coffee beans to produce an incredibly strong, thick and dark coffee.
The Vietnamese people know how to utilize what nature has provided them. As the biggest producer of Robusta coffee, the locals roast the coffee beans with butter to prepare a delicious cup of thick coffee.
Vietnamese coffee can be served in two major ways. The *ca Phe sua da* (iced coffee with sweetened condensed milk) or *ca phe da* (iced black coffee). In case you don't specify your coffee, the waiter is likely to serve you the *ca phe sua da* with four to five tea spoons of sugar.

Typical ca phe sua da

In addition to sweetened milk, local Vietnamese coffee may be served with eggs, butter, yoghurt and cheese. For instance, in Giang Café in Hanoi, visitors enjoy the area's famous coffee where egg yolks, coffee powder, condensed milk and cheese are mixed together to produce a robust coffee.

When touring Hanoi at night, you're likely to find the local Vietnamese people on the streets or in cafes drinking coffee while talking to each other. The coffee is mostly served in small cups called **phins.** The coffee can either be brewed on your presence or you may find already brewed coffee waiting to be consumed.

Pho noodles and beef

Pho noodle is the staple food of Vietnam people and is mostly served with beef or chicken meat at any time of the day. Pho noodles date back to mid-1880s during the French and Chinese colonial era. Most spices used were imported from China while the French introduced red meat as an additional ingredient in the recipe. Since then, Pho noodles and beef became the national dish of Vietnam attracting people from the west who tremendously fell in love with the deceptive simplicity and the complex delicious flavors.

Typical Pho noodle with beef

During the Second World War, Vietnam was divided into North and South Vietnam. The North which was a communist country selected Hanoi as its capital while the South which was democracy centered selected Saigon as its capital. Most people fled from the North to the South to avoid the communist rule taking with them the Pho noodle recipes. Unlike in the North, the South had abundant herbs and other ingredients which led to the revolution of the pho noodle.

Shortly after 1954, conflicts were sparked up by the communist countries (Soviet Union and China) who supported the North while United States supported the democratic South. From 1963 to 1973, the Vietnam War broke out which led to the fall of Saigon. Most refugee families fled to neighboring countries such as Philippines, Malaysia and Indonesia while others were accepted in the United States, Australia and European countries.

Although the Vietnamese pho noodle underwent some revolution after most families fled Saigon, I will share with you the original pho noodles of the local Vietnamese people served with beef.

Ingredients include;

- 5 pounds of beef marrow
- 2 pieces of ginger
- 2 yellow onions
- ¼ cup fish sauce
- 3 tablespoons of sugar
- 1 tablespoon of sea salt
- 6 whole cloves
- 10 whole star anise
- 1 pound of 1/16 inch rice sticks
- ⅓ cup chopped cilantro
- 10 sprigs Asian basil
- Black pepper
- 1 serrano chili

Preparation

Place a large pot on high heat then add your beef marrow. Season it with salt and pepper then leave it for about 5-6 minutes. Transfer the meat to a plate then add the onions and ginger to the pot and leave it to cook for about 4 minutes. Add the broth, three cups of water and cinnamon. Reduce the heat then leave it to cook for about 30 minutes to 1 hour. Meanwhile, transfer the beef to a bowl of cold water to prevent it from drying up. Add the fish sauce to the broth and discard the ginger and cinnamon stick. When your dish is ready to serve, divide the noodles into four bowls with the broth at the top then beef, scallions, cilantro, bean sprouts and onions.

Final Words

There are lots of other things which visitors can enjoy once they go to Vietnam. There are hundreds of things to do, lots of local food to eat and drink as well as local festivals which reveals the country's origin and history since the 1st century AD. After reading this book I believe that you have a general idea of what Vietnam has to offer.
If you are planning your trip it's important to be aware of holidays in Vietnam. You can watch a list of holidays in Vietnam here.

Thank you for purchasing this book. If you enjoyed this book, kindly take your time to write a short review about it. It really helps me out.

Thank you!

Printed in Great Britain
by Amazon